BRITAIN IN OLD PHOTOGRAPHS

KIRKBY & DISTRICT
A SECOND SELECTION

FRANK ASHLEY, SYLVIA SINFIELD & GERALD LEE

SUTTON PUBLISHING LIMITED

Sutton Publishing Limited
Phoenix Mill · Thrupp · Stroud
Gloucestershire · GL5 2BU

First published 1997

Copyright © Frank Ashley, Sylvia Sinfield &
Gerald Lee, 1997

Cover photographs: *front*: Kirkby's thirteenth-
century Cross; *back*: Celebration of the
Queen's Coronation.
Title page: Headgear pulleys being changed,
Annesley Colliery, 1954.

British Library Cataloguing in Publication Data
A catalogue record for this book is available from the
British Library.

ISBN 0-7509-1658-3

Typeset in 10/12 Perpetua.
Typesetting and origination by
Sutton Publishing Limited.
Printed in Great Britain by
Ebenezer Baylis, Worcester.

CONTENTS

Station Street, pictured here in the early 1980s, has changed its face a good deal over the years. Some of the old buildings have gone (houses once stood where the shops are on the right of the picture), businesses have been modernized, trees planted and pavements widened. When Kirkby's planners of long ago built this thoroughfare they could never in their wildest fancies have imagined the vast amount of traffic with which the street would one day have to cope.

This and the following five pictures (pages 9–11) are all the work of Grimm. Here, looking north-east we see the church and rectory. Just to the west of the church, we are told, once stood Kirkby Castle.

One wonders what significance there was in this Sunday morning procession in 1775. All those on parade seem to be of uniform height and in identical dress.

The church and Manor House. Built in 1622 the great house of Kirkby was unfortunately demolished in 1964.

A view epitomizing Kirkby's agricultural past. This view is of one of the many substantial farms there were in those expansive days.

Samuel Grimm was a friend of Sir Richard Kaye, incumbent of St Wilfrid's from 1765 to 1810, and was a frequent visitor to the rectory. The artist wrote of this picturesque part of long-vanished Kirkby, 'View from my apartment'.

East of the church. The rectory is adjacent, and the line of buildings continues along Church Street.

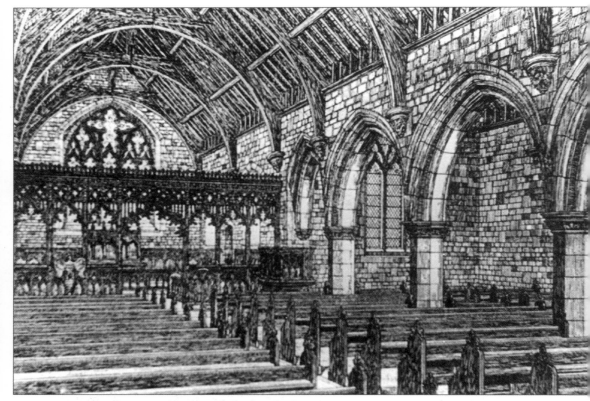

It was a new beginning for St Wilfrid's after the fire of 1907. This is a drawing of the proposed interior submitted by Louis Ambler, FRIBA, then the architect for the Southwell Diocese.

"I was glad when they said unto me, we will go into the House of the Lord."

This was drawn especially for the church's first funding campaign in 1963 and used ever since. The artists fee was ½ lb of tobacco.

WITH SHINING MORNING FACE

Now Kingsway County Primary, this school, pictured in 1928, has over the years provided for various age ranges of both boys and girls. There have been some memorable headteachers, none more so than Mr Nowell who, sixty years ago, whatever the weather, walked daily from his home at Nuncargate.

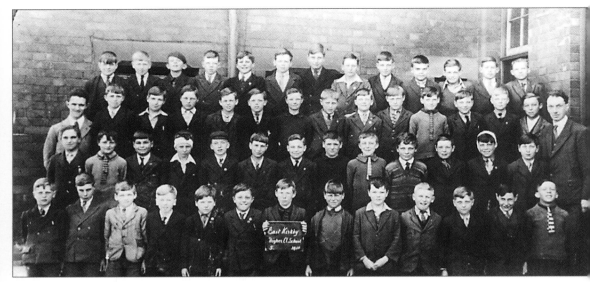

East Kirkby Higher Grade School, Class 5, 1930. They are smartly turned out in spite of the two bandaged casualties on the second row from the front. Mr Garnet, headmaster, is on the right.

Kingsway Senior Boys, 1948. Standing on the left is the headmaster, Mr Cox. On the right is Mr Ron Allin, accomplished pianist, who for years put the boys through their musical paces.

East Kirkby Council Infants, 1920s. There is not the faintest glimmer of a smile.

Kingsway School, 1935. The hall has been decorated for the Silver Jubilee of King George V and Queen Mary.

Standard 2, East Kirkby Infants School, 1926.

A class of Annesley School, 1928. Headmaster, James Herbert, stands on the right.

A class at East Kirkby School, *c.* 1910. Stiff Eton collars were obviously in fashion then, but two lads on the left of the photograph look somewhat conscious of their lace neckwear.

Boys from Kingsway School pause on their instructional country walk at Fryer's Farm, *c.* 1940. The railway wagons on the embankment are for use at Bentinck Colliery.

Two boys admiring the Royal Coat of Arms at Kirkby Hardwick, *c.* 1950. The historic house was built and fortified during the Wars of the Roses. It was in possession of the Shrewsbury family in 1530 when Cardinal Wolsey stayed there one night on his ill-fated journey from York to London, having been ordered to return to the capital to face a charge of treason on the instruction of King Henry VIII.

The Coat of Arms was erected in 1597 by Sir Charles Cavendish, in residence at the time. Unfortunately, when Kirkby Hardwick was demolished in the late 1960s the Coat of Arms mysteriously disappeared.

Is the smile of the boy on the right of the picture because he has noticed the moustache on the lion's face?

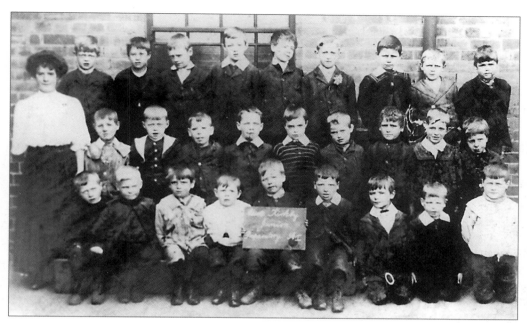

The Preparatory Class, East Kirkby Junior School, 1910. Serious it undoubtedly was, but one lad on the back row is sporting a buttonhole for the occasion.

Morven Park Primary School, a landmark of Kirkby for as long as people can remember; it gave the name, not very imaginatively, to School Street, which cuts through to Diamond Avenue.

Orchard Infants of thirty years ago have just performed their Nativity Play. Every member of the class was involved and happily they all assembled for their curtain call.

East Kirkby Infants, 1930. The boys are vastly outnumbered by the girls.

Waiting to cross at the corner of Lowmoor Road before the erection of traffic lights here. The restraining hand of Mr Hughes, Kirkby's first crossing patrolman, is at the ready, with the law keeping a watchful eye on the proceedings.

A group of schoolboys standing against the remains of the Cavendish Wall on Marrot Hill, Kirkby Woodhouse, *c.* 1930. It was on this site that Sir Charles Cavendish had intended to build his house in 1597, but after a skirmish with Sir John Stanhope and his followers he abandoned the project. Of the wall in the photograph there is now no trace.

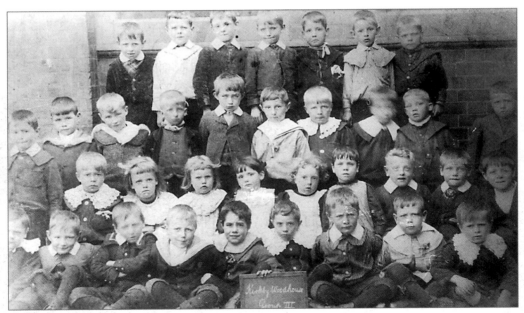

Group III, Kirkby Woodhouse School, almost ninety years ago. Another collection of infants with suspicious expressions and fancy neckwear.

Girls of Class IIIA at Vernon Road School, 1936. The teacher, seated midway along the second row, is Miss Elsie Turner. She was also the school music and choir mistress.

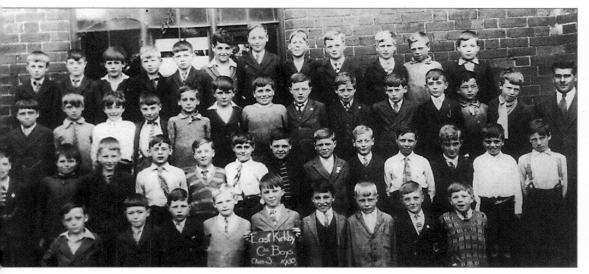

East Kirkby Boys School, Class 3, 1930. The teacher is Mr H. Smith.

May Day with the juniors. The top photograph, showing enthusiastic bows and curtsies, was taken on the field behind Chapel Street School in 1954. The lower photograph, in the school playground, is of the 1961 celebration, the signal to start dancing eagerly awaited.

Church Street Infants, 1928. The headmistress, the redoubtable Miss Lilian Quinion, stands on the left, with teacher Miss Dickinson on the right. Facing the camera, it seems, is still a major hazard.

Church Street Infants four years later. Miss Kate Sharman, aunt of cricketing legend Harold Larwood, is the teacher. It was a solemn business, of course, for these young musicians to hold their poses, and the conductor, in the centre of the back row, obviously takes her responsibilities very seriously.

A class at Jeffries Junior School, 1964/5. Headmaster, Fred Hill, is standing on the right. At about this time, when the pupils of Mowlands School off Sutton Road were relocated, juniors went to Jeffries and seniors to the new Kirkby Comprehensive School.

May Day again, this time with the Merry Men of Sherwood, *c.* 1960.

A LESS FRANTIC AGE

Annesley Colliery Miners Welfare, early 1920s. The gentleman in the centre is the steward, Frank Sturman. The building was substantially altered in 1932 by the addition of a ballroom and concert hall. It became a very popular centre of entertainment.

Bearing little resemblance to the Annesley Park we know today, this photograph was taken in about 1900 by the noted local photographer, H.G. Owston. It shows Home Farm Corner, on the right, and the old Toll Bar Cottage, offering a peep into what we fondly imagine to be an idyllic past.

The fishing lodge, Annesley Park, early 1900s. Charming it may have looked, but it afforded its tenant little in the way of modern amenities. The old building was one of a number on the Annesley Estate demolished after the Second World War.

St Wilfrid's rectory was built in 1717 and is shown on this photograph before the removal of the west wing. Matthew Brailsford, rector of the parish 1703–34, wrote, after making alterations to the house, 'It is the most commodious dwelling that any parson in the county hath.'

Mrs Chaworth-Musters opens the 1956 garden party. Seated are Mrs Lunn, the Revd E.W.G. Lunn, rector 1954–60, and churchwardens Bellamy and Hardy.

The interior of the Mother Church of the parish before the fire of January 1907. This strikingly simple arch was replaced at the rebuilding by a fine wooden screen carved *in situ* at the entrance to the chancel.

Kingsway Park about forty years ago. Shrubs and flower beds abound in ordered profusion, and there is not a vandalized bench in sight.

Sixty years ago this three-wheeler car no doubt cut a dash through Kirkby's streets. It is shown, arousing some curiosity, in the yard of the Nag's Head.

Chapel Street, when there was still a rural air about this part of Kirkby. The house behind the bystanders was the home of the farming Mycroft family. The farmhouse was later demolished and the land used for part of the filling station forecourt. Beyond is the Waggon and Horses, and farther along a number of fine old stone houses, some of which are still there. The building on the right was part of Brailsford's corner. Note the gas lamp and the boy sauntering up the centre of the street.

Three lively lads at Kirkby's thirteenth-century Cross. It is thought the Cross has been in place since 1218, some years before the village was granted a market and fair.

The Revd James Butterwick, rector of St Wilfrid's from 1899 to 1920, and one-time chaplain at Welbeck Abbey. This photograph was taken in the rectory garden shortly after his induction.

Mr and Mrs Cyril Sargent, two of Kirkby's prominent residents, photographed against Fryer's Mill shortly after the First World War. Mr Sargent is now approaching his 100th year.

Kingsway, 1938. This imposing road, renamed after the visit of King George V and Queen Mary in 1929, is hardly ever free of traffic, leading as it does from the Shoulder of Mutton Hill to Kirkby's main crossroads. The arch on the left is the south entrance to Kingsway Park. Over the archway it is recorded that the park was opened in 1930.

The Forty-four Steps, climbed over the years by countless walkers making their way from Mayfield, Bentinck and Old Kirkby towards Portland Park.

Wilfred, Doris and John Mattley in the garden of Owston, the Annesley Woodhouse photographer. The year is 1913, and this photograph recalls an age when musical evenings were a popular form of entertainment. The Mattley brothers and sister were accomplished violinists.

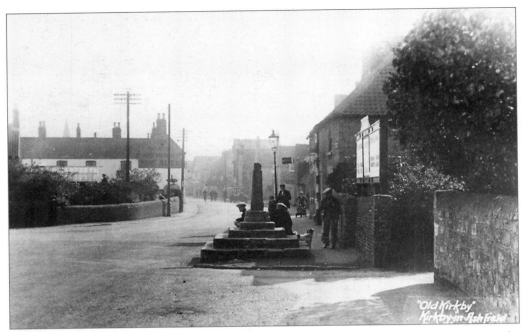

Kirkby Cross, 1938. The Cross was then a regular meeting place. The Green Man, no longer there, is the building on the left. Walking and cycling were the chief means of travel, and high sodium street lighting was some years away. The posters on the board behind the Cross advertise forthcoming attractions at the local cinemas.

Away from the madding crowd, a young man poses for the photographer beside Fryer's Mill pond, c. 1920.

A quiet drink at the Nag's Head, 1954. Mr Penney, the licensee, serves some of his regulars. The notice just visible on the left firmly states the pub's policy: 'Tapping and borrowing strictly forbidden.'

Taking it easy after a spell with the heavy roller. Hardly the clothing favoured by youngsters of today, but then, the photograph was taken eighty years ago, close to Fryer's Mill.

Skegby Road, Annesley Woodhouse, during the First World War. Children and friends from the farmyard pose for the photographer. The General Havelock public house is the far building on the right.

Obviously a nature lesson as two young companions walk through Portland Park towards the end of the year, c. 1970.

Mr and Mrs John Musters. John Musters of Colwick Hall was, in his time, a famed sportsman; his wife, formerly Mary Chaworth of Annesley Hall, was Byron's boyhood love, and is immortalized in the lines:

> Now no more, the hours beguiling,
> Former favourite haunts I see,
> Now no more my Mary smiling
> Makes ye seem a heaven to me.

Annesley Hall and part of the grounds, around which Byron and Mary strolled, c. 1910. Sadly, this fine old house was seriously damaged by suspected arson as recently as late summer 1997.

The Blocks, Annesley. More respectfully named the Grove Cottages, they provided a vantage point on at least two Royal occasions. On 11 September 1904 King Edward VII and Queen Alexandra passed along the road by car. Ten years later, on 24 June 1914, so did King George V and Queen Mary, on their way to the Dukeries.

An unusual tree in Portland Park that has exercised the curiosity of many walkers. It is called the Bear's Cave, the name no doubt causing wide-eyed youngsters in a more tranquil age to hurry by.

MINING MEMORIES

Newstead's first shafts were sunk in 1874, and for 113 years — until 1987 — the pit had continuously high production. In the years 1959 to 1975/6 a million tons per year was topped sixteen times, with a record 1,285,461 tons mined in 1966/67.

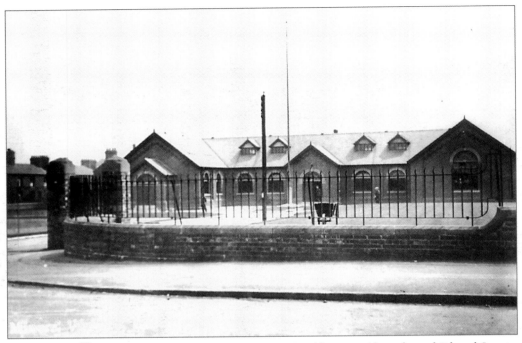

East Kirkby Miners' Welfare buildings fronting Lowmoor Road between Alexandra and Edward Streets, and facing Summit Colliery. The 'Welfare', built in 1923, was hugely popular in its day. This picture is from a card sent home by one of the Welsh miners who came to work in Kirkby after the 1926 strike.

Sunshine and shadows as members of the Welfare line up with colliery officials, 1950. In the centre of the group is that year's Coal Queen.

Summit Colliery was for more than eighty years a vital part of Kirkby, at one time employing more than 1,500 men. Shortly before its closure well in excess of a million tons were mined in one year. Work ceased in 1969 and the colliery became a casualty of the district's mining history.

A ground-level shot of Summit Colliery in the early part of the century, when much of the local transportation was by horse and cart.

A meal at the Hill 60 Club. Named after a place of First World War action, this club, situated on Church Hill, and always well patronized by miners, still has a strong and lively membership.

Headgear pulleys being changed at Annesley Colliery, 1954. Many years of coal production lay ahead for one of the area's busiest pits.

Quiet settles over Newstead Colliery and village in 1988, a year after the colliery was closed.

Happier times for Newstead when the pit was still in full production, early 1970s.

One of the last working shifts at Newstead Colliery before the pit closed in 1987.

Bentinck Colliery in its heyday. In the foreground is Fryer's Mill dam. Across the road to the left is Fryer's Farm. The mill, long demolished, is still remembered by elderly local residents. A mill was first built beside the dam in the latter part of the eighteenth century, rebuilt about 100 years later, and remained in the Fryer family until the 1930s, the tenancy eventually passing to Mr William Curtis, a well-known Kirkby butcher.

Annesley Colliery and village. This photograph was taken in the 1930s, when testing times were ahead. The outlook for mining was bleak; in 1932 output was the lowest recorded for thirty-four years. Work at the pits was more irregular than for a generation past and there was a further heavy reduction in the number employed in the industry. With the outbreak of the Second World War, however, demand for coal increased, and for many years afterwards mining flourished. Sadly, that is no longer the case, but when this photograph was taken King Coal had still many productive years to reign.

Bentinck Miners Welfare, Sutton Road, *c.* 1950. Much in use still, but then the centre of the Bentinck Colliery sports complex. Beyond, to the left, was the cricket ground, one of the most attractive in the county, and further along, a much-used football ground. Behind the Welfare were tennis courts and bowling greens.

Looks of eager anticipation as, fifty years ago, a party of Leg o' Mutton regulars prepares to set off on a day's outing. The popular pub was then situated in Byron Street.

CO-OPERATIVELY & SWEET REMINDERS

The first shop of Kirkby Folly Equitable Co-operative Society, 1890. Situated on Lowmoor Road, the records state 'That we engage Mr Abbott as Manager on his own terms of £1 2s per week, to be advanced as the sales will allow'.

The Central Stores, built by Sharley of Kirkby, for £546. The premises were opened on 15 October 1892 by Mr Henry Lewis, a silver key being presented to him by Mr Hind, the architect. A tea was provided in the Primitive Methodist schoolroom and music for the occasion was played by the Annesley Brass Band.

Suitable premises for the first butchering business in Pond Street, East Kirkby, were purchased for the sum of £292 10s, and the shop was opened on 22 November 1896. The first butcher appointed was Mr F. Smith of Langley Mill.

The Kirkby Hill Branch, built on a piece of land bought on 23 November 1896. The land had an area of 344 square yards and the purchase price was 6s per yard. The new stores were built in 1897 for £650, and were opened in 1898.

Above: Increasing business meant that additional space was required. The property adjoining the Central Stores was bought in November 1898 for £600, enabling rebuilding and expansion to take place. The result was a splendid new building including grocery, footwear, hardware, drapery, butchery and greengrocery departments. In addition, there were offices and an Education Department on the upper floor. The premises served generations of Kirkby shoppers.

Left: Following the success of the Hill Branch, a shop was opened on Church Street, in Old Kirkby, and became No. 3 Branch of the growing local society.

Some of the officers and committee of the Co-operative Society. Back row, left to right: G.H. Hunt, J.R. Hunt, J.F. Fearn, J. Pitchford, T. Mills, G. Godfrey. Front row: J.G. Shacklock (general secretary), G. Varnum, C.T. Pilch (vice-president), W.A. Wells (president), W. Coleman (treasurer), J. Wright.

Education Committee. Back row, left to right: J.G. Shacklock, C. Bryan, T. Mills. Front row: W. Frith, J. Abbott, H. Marsh. Already plans were in hand to show that 'the co-operative movement is a moral as well as a material one. Increased comfort, happier homes, nobler ideals, trust in, and a higher sense of duty to, fellow men, are amongst its aims.'

Almost fifty years ago Martins: Makers of Good Sweets moved from their original Southwell Lane premises to a modern factory off Wheatley Avenue. This is a picture of the busy general office.

Highly productive methods by the standards of the day; the girls are paying strict attention to their wrapping machines.

A section of the works devoted to product examination and strict quality control.

In their distinctive jars, Buttermints — Prince of Peppermints are packed before despatch to the far corners of the British Isles and overseas.

The Despatch Department with, on the right, chargehand Ted Rush. As will be seen from the crates, this consignment is destined for the NAAFI in Benghazi and Dar-es-Salaam.

The Engineering Shop with, from left to right, Messrs Bancroft, Butler, Overfield and Stafford.

A recent view of the south end of Southwell Lane. In the middle distance on the left is the filled-in Central railway cutting, while on the right are manufacturing units, a car repair business and a hosiery factory, together occupying buildings that were once the first Martin's works.

There came the day when Martin's Sweets was sold and the factory turned over to hosiery production. Mr Malcolm Martin (far right), son of the founder, an engineer by inclination and training, set up his own firm near the old factory. Malcolm Martin Engineering specialized in mining products and the building of trucks that at one time were in great demand.

SPORTING PRINTS

St Thomas' Cricket Club, a hundred years ago. One of the best of the local sides, the club went by coach and charabanc to play far and wide in the county. Back row, left to right: A. Allen (scorer), A. Kemp, J. Hufton, F. Bostock, G. Taylor, F. Lee and J. Gubbins (umpire). Middle row: G. Hilton, J. Smith, H. Toon (captain), W. Roberts, A. Shacklock. Front row: J. Shacklock, B. Glossop, G. Peach.

A sporting evening at the Waggon and Horses on the occasion of Nottingham Forest's promotion to Division One, 1977. On the extreme right Kirkby businessman, John Wheatley, shakes hands with the landlord, Cyril Vigors. Looking on are members of the Forest team and the pub team, The Waggoners.

Kirkby Park Cricket Club, 1932. Standing, left to right: L. Tompkins, I. Frith, R. Brown, E. Ellis, W. Whitehurst. Front row: W. Townsend, C. Salt, L. Wood, S. Shacklock, E. Brown, A. Woolley. From this early group, taken soon after the club was formed, fine sides developed, and earned the accolade, *Kirkby Park – Kirkby's Pride*.

A social gathering of committee members, friends and players of Kirkby Park, 1950s. The venue was the Sherwood House Inn.

Nuncargate Cricket Club, almost fifty years ago, on the ground behind the Cricketers' Arms, having just won the Kirkby Charity Cup. It was with Nuncargate that Larwood began his illustrious cricketing career.

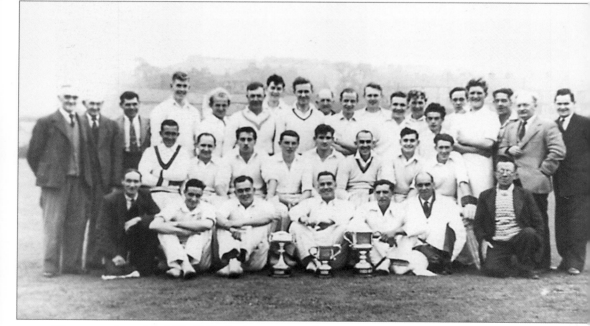

Nuncargate 1st and 2nd XI, 1950s. In those postwar days there was a proliferation of fine sides in Kirkby and district. Nuncar (the name was often shortened) could always win a trophy or two.

Kirkby LMS FC, May 1947. By no means all the players were railwaymen.

Built in 1834, this building was a Methodist chapel on what was once Town Street, and later Chapel Street. For at least sixty years, however, it has been a billiards and snooker hall, allowing stars in the making to practise their game.

A youthful Harold Larwood, who was to play 300 matches for Nottinghamshire, take 1,247 wickets, and become the scourge of batsmen throughout his career. He settled in Australia after the Second World War (strange, perhaps, after the bodyline storm) but his popularity never diminished either at home or in his adopted country.

During the 1960s and early '70s it was open house once a month at St Wilfrid's Rectory for the Men's Fellowship. Many and varied were the personalities who accepted invitations to address the members. On this occasion, and enjoying the refreshments prepared by the rector's wife, the speaker was John Whetton, famous Olympic athlete (second from the right).

The Mowlands School cricket team with teacher Ken Smith, 1958. On the left can be seen the Nissen huts, used as classrooms until they were demolished some years later after the children had gone on to other schools. Situated at the top of George Street the Nissen huts were built during the war to accommodate Bevin Boys who came to Kirkby to work in the local mines.

Tommy Lawtons, Larwoods and Hardstaffs in the making? Morven Park School football and cricket teams, 1947. From the look of them they all fancy their chances. Headmaster, Mr Mollart, is on the left in both photographs, and, strangely, it is an earlier Ken Smith who is the teacher.

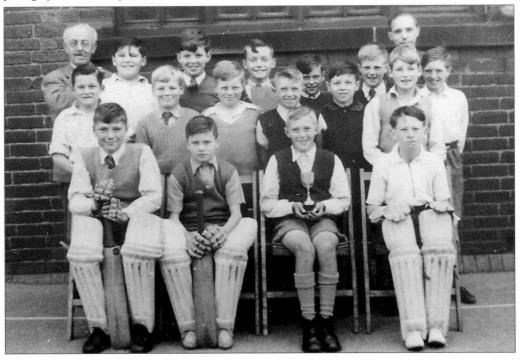

DISASTER & AFTER AT PORTLAND PARK

A summer's morning showing the warden's cottage at Portland Park, built more than sixty years ago.

A corner of the old visitor centre. A group examine the wall posters, of which there was an impressive collection, and browse through the albums of local interest. Much irreplaceable memorabilia was lost in the fire.

Resting awhile outside the old centre. The gentleman on the right is 'Portland' Bill Smith, keen conservationist, who has done much to instruct and entertain the Portland Park Youth Group with his knowledge of, and interest in, this part of Kirkby.

The devastation that greeted conservationists on the morning of Sunday 18 October 1992. The fire broke out in the early hours of the morning. Although the firemen fought valiantly to limit the damage, little of the visitor centre and its contents could be saved. The cause of the fire remains unknown.

So much time and endeavour had been reduced to nought in a few short hours.

Nothing could more effectively illustrate the will to overcome the difficulties than this photograph and the next. Stunned supporters have gathered to take stock of the situation. A touch of wry humour is shown by the ground-level visitor centre board.

Word spread quickly and walkers came. It was close to the end of British Summer Time so a warming cup of tea had to be available.

One of the first tasks after the fire was to provide a temporary under-cover visitor centre. An effort had to be made to prevent sombre realism turning into unrelieved gloom.

Welcome music to revive the spirits. Kirkby Colliery Welfare Band provides a much-needed interlude and helps to raise funds. In the photograph below, Mr and Mrs Arthur Russ, now retired after being in business in Kirkby for many years, rest during the concert interval.

Owls from Sheila Cohen's bird rescue centre provide two young visitors with a brief diversion. The Park is an area rich in flora and fauna and offers much to those interested in the changing seasons.

Tony Gamblin offers a snack to Cyril the Squirrel. Cyril was a long-time resident of Portland Park and tame enough to mingle with visitors.

The new visitor centre, completed in October 1994. This imposing building was made possible through generous financial help from the European Community, the Countryside Commission, Ashfield District Council and the Kirkby and District Conservation Society.

In 1914 the Duke and Duchess of Portland celebrated their Silver Wedding and the 21st birthday of their son. The Duke wrote to the then chairman of Kirkby Council: 'To mark these happy events I trust you will do us the honour of accepting on behalf of the parishioners, a gift.' The gift was Portland Park.

Portland Park – still the Quarries to older Kirkby people – is a haven for flora and fauna that offers something of interest to its many visitors from January to December. Hundreds visit the Park in the course of a year. It has a special place in the hearts of local conservationists, who put in time and effort to preserve the tranquil acres of walks and woodlands.

A SALUTE TO STEAM

Photographed heading north, this specially chartered Pullman train, hauled by Silver Link and hired by the Ian Allan organization, graced the Kirkby track in 1956. Such star engines usually kept to the national lines.

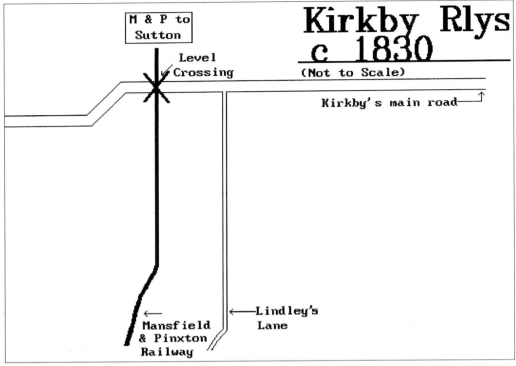

Kirkby Rlys c 1830

(Not to Scale)

M & P to Sutton

Level Crossing

Kirkby's main road →

← Mansfield & Pinxton Railway

← Lindley's Lane

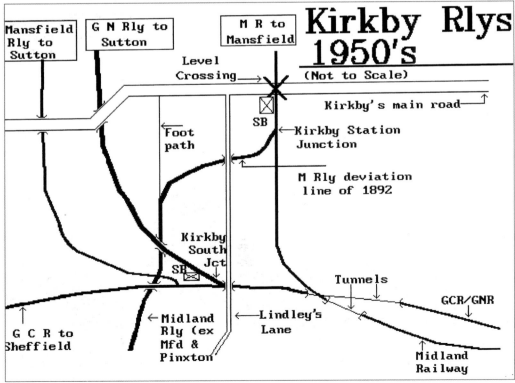

Kirkby Rlys 1950's

(Not to Scale)

Mansfield Rly to Sutton

G N Rly to Sutton

M R to Mansfield

Level Crossing →

Kirkby's main road →

SB

← Kirkby Station Junction

M Rly deviation line of 1892

Foot path

Kirkby South Jct

SB

Tunnels

GCR/GNR

G C R to Sheffield

← Midland Rly (ex Mfd & Pinxton

← Lindley's Lane

Midland Railway

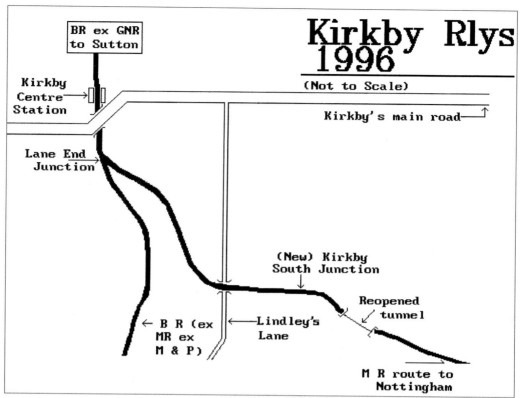

These three maps span 166 years of railways in Kirkby. It is interesting to compare the busy network of the 1950s with the Mansfield & Pinxton Railway of more than a century previously and with the new layout of today.

Class 3 40079 Worksop–Nottingham train heading for Kirkby tunnel, Kingsway Park border, c. 1955.

A Bank Holiday excursion, Matlock-bound, 1954. These engines were nicknamed 'Crabs' by the men who had to work them, on account of their ungainly appearance.

This K2-class locomotive has just brought its train past Kirkby police station. The house in the distance pinpoints the position, close to the new junction of the Robin Hood line at Lane End.

The Annesley end of Kirkby tunnel. The tunnel was 199 yd long, and was driven in about 1848.

No. 90202, an 'Austerity' locomotive, pulls a train of trucks loaded with small coal, no doubt destined for a power station further down the line.

One of the 'Tankies' of the ex-Great Eastern railway, No. 69654 is climbing away from Kirkby South Junction towards the Central station and on to Mansfield.

Passenger working over the Mansfield line just after the Second World War was largely by ex-Great Northern locomotives, but after one left the track near Clipstone and fell from the embankment, these class A5s were brought in to replace them. No. 69809 is seen crossing the bridge over the Mansfield & Pinxton route on its way to the tunnel and to Nottingham.

Expresses steaming through Kirkby Bentinck station were a daily occurrence. This class B1 locomotive is bound for Sheffield and Manchester.

A Sunday in June 1953. Kirkby South Junction was handed over to civil engineering to allow for the whole of the pointwork to be relaid. June was chosen so advantage could be taken of maximum daylight in order that the huge task could be completed in time for Monday's services. Tremendous manual labour was involved, with only the steam crane to help with the lifting.

Following withdrawal of passenger trains on the Mansfield line, a very short-lived service was introduced from Nottingham to the Great Northern Railway station at Outram Street, Sutton. This photograph was taken in 1956.

A heavy freighter struggles with its train of coal. The driver is using his sanders (equipment to direct a jet of steam to blow dried sand between the driving wheels and the rails) to get a grip on the track alongside Lowmoor Road.

St Wilfrid's Church rises indistinctly in the distance as loco No. 63922 lifts a mixed freight train from Bentinck station towards the long Annesley tunnel. The elevated line behind the train sweeps right towards Kirkby Central.

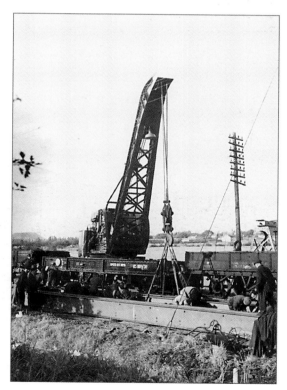

The line near Grive's Lane crossing is having steel girders laid beneath the sleepers, September 1952. This enabled winter floodwater to be drained away and the Kingsway estate to be built on the fields behind the crane.

Empty wagons bound for Summit Colliery, 1954. No doubt there was some explaining to be done as to how the left-hand buffer came to be damaged.

An early locomotive is ready for work in the Summit yard, July 1898. The pit and loco were both owned by the Butterley Co.

Part of the LMS line. The distant bridge near the police station is now awaiting strengthening.

Locomotive No. 40184 on the once much-used Nottingham–Worksop passenger service. It is shown traversing the Summit crossing under the iron bridge that daily resounded to pit boots when the gates were closed.

There were no regular passenger services provided on the Mansfield & Pinxton line, but around 1832 the proprietors of the Boat Inn at Pinxton ran a four-wheeled horse-drawn coach once a week from Pinxton to Mansfield on market days. This illustration comes from a Buxton water-colour now owned by Mansfield Museum and Art Gallery.

Loads of steel plate and tubes brought down the Mansfield line, no doubt manufactured in the Sheffield area. These class 02 locomotives were originally built for the Great Northern Railway.

No. 43940 is making for the Kirkby shed after dropping its empty wagons – a familiar sight in the bustling railway/mining days. On the left is the control office. Summit Colliery (slag heaps visible on the skyline) is working flat out in the background.

This train is made up of empty fish vans, and after its passage no one was left in any doubt of its contents. Southbound, the train passes through Bentinck station.

Stretching back under the two LNER bridges, the train waits with its empty wagons for clearance from the signalman to be set back into the Bentinck Colliery sidings, 1951.

Taken from Lindley's Lane bridge, this photograph shows the layout of Kirkby South Junction. The Great Northern Railway bears right towards Police Station Hill; the Mansfield line swings right beyond the signal-box. The train is carrying a load of Kirkby's then staple product, coal.

The evening express freight train from Mansfield runs along the edge of Kingsway Park, *c.* 1951. Summit Colliery tip is in the far distance on the left.

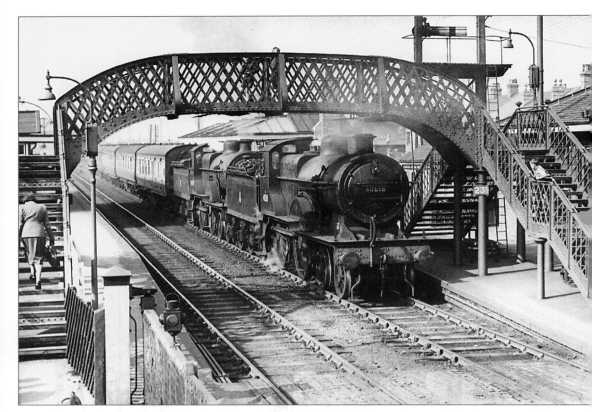

This Saturday double-header is a Worksop–Nottingham train, 1953. How many of us at some time have stood on the bridge, as the two lads are doing, hoping to get enveloped in the fog of the exhaust steam as the train passed underneath? And how many trips were made over the bridge in the course of a year when the crossing gates were closed?

THE CHANGING SCENE

Pipe renewal at the corner of Portland Street and Lowmoor Road, 1954/55. As usual, a group takes interest in operations.

The King's cinema, which opened in 1912, had what can best be described as a chequered existence. In its 'silent' days it had seating for 600 until a balcony was added in 1919. There was at one time a lengthy closure; then talkies took over and it became as popular as the Regent and the Star. With films, live turns and concerts (under the management of Alf Wall it enjoyed a very flourishing period) it entertained Kirkby until 1962. In the top picture partial demolition is underway to transform the cinema into a garage and filling station. The filling station has now gone and other commercial enterprises have recently been tried on this site.

Morley Street looking towards Station Street, early 1980s. The houses on the left were shortly to be demolished to make way for the new Youth and Community Centre. The Salvation Army Citadel, on the near right, remains.

'The House That Serves You Best' proclaim the notices in both windows of Cupit's shop, for years established on Lowmoor Road, selling pots, pans and miscellaneous hardware. Mrs Cupit is photographed outside the shop fifty years ago.

Byron Street from Lowmoor Road in the late 1950s, well before demolition and the building of Kirkby Precinct. Woodhead's provision stores is the shop on the left, Pounder's Shoes on the right.

A view from high up on Tennyson Street showing the old Market Hall and Walker's factory. The Market Hall made way for the Festival Hall; Walker's became a spring factory. The licensed premises on the corner of Hodgkinson Road were once owned by an old professional cricketer known, in fact, as Cricketer Clarke.

Southwell Lane looking towards Summit Colliery shortly after the Second World War. Up to that time this part of the lane ran between Speed's Farm, garden allotments and fields. All that was to change dramatically in a few short years.

To cope with the postwar lack of building materials prefabricated dwellings were erected. Pictured is one of the original Kirkby prefabs on Elm Tree Road, leading off Southwell Lane. It was stated at the time that prefabs were expected to last ten years, but many were much older than that before they were replaced.

As supplies eased, building continued apace and, with the later development of industrial estates when Summit Colliery closed, Southwell Lane became one of the busiest secondary roads in Kirkby. This view shows the lane's transformation. Keen gardeners once tended their plots where the houses stand on the left.

Kirkby Central station on a snowy day just before closure on the last day of 1955. In its heyday this station was serviced by more than twenty passenger trains a day, and by far more carrying freight.

Above, Diamond Avenue, *c.* 1910. Trinity Methodist Church, much altered, is still there in the photograph below, taken in about 1980, as are most of the houses. The cottages in the top right foreground were demolished many years ago, and the days are long gone when walkers could wander without danger on the road. Diamond Avenue leads to Nail Nest Hill, 636 ft above sea level.

A car approaches the top of the Shoulder of Mutton Hill. There is a plaque on the house at the top of the hill which states the location is the highest point in the county. (Residents of Huthwaite are inclined to disagree.) Reynolds Stores, the Old Smithy and Kirkby Church of Christ were once notable landmarks along this part of the road.

Welbeck Street, 1910. These houses are typical of the period. At this time not all streets had the smooth surfaces we know today.

The Four Lane Ends, Kirkby, late 1940s. This road junction is shown before traffic lights were installed, and before it was compulsory for motor-cyclists to wear crash helmets. Then, as now, it was the busiest place in town, but at the time of the photograph it could never have been visualized that there would one day be almost non-stop traffic.

The upper part of Chapel Street, long one of the most picturesque parts of Old Kirkby, *c.* 1955. Broom Cottage, on the immediate right, was demolished to make way for a carpet warehouse and forecourt, but the creepered house is still there, as is the Waggon and Horses beyond it. The old-style phone box is now a listed building.

After passing through Annesley Park the traveller was greeted by old Badger Box. The well-known public house has moved its location a few yards from the corner. Note the bus timetable hanging on the wall, and the line across the road, used, before the erection of traffic lights, to warn of the major road ahead.

The Lodge, Annesley Park, *c.* 1910. Note the open tourer car ready to be driven on the then quiet roads surrounding the park.

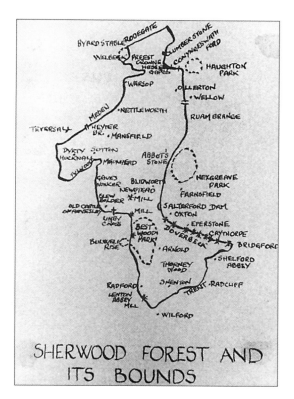

SHERWOOD FOREST AND ITS BOUNDS

A map showing the haunts of Robin Hood and his Merry Men, stretching from the River Trent in the south to the northern boundaries of the Dukeries, and, from Bridgford in the east to Hucknall and Teversall near the Derbyshire border.

A train has just gone through Kirkby LMS station on its way down to Pye Bridge, and the signalman has obviously got to attend to some minor difficulty manually. Delay at this crossing was an accepted fact of life in Kirkby, whatever the reason.

Bateman's Yard, Church Street, one of the many yards that once gave the street much of its fascination. It has retained a great deal of its character, blending the old and the new. The building on the immediate right, formerly Church Street post office, dates from 1738.

The 1980s brought a determined effort to give a new image to much of Kirkby. Here a well-known part of Lowmoor Road is shown in the early stages of demolition.

New Street, shown here as it was in 1965, has been totally demolished. In place of the old houses, some of which had character, there are now modern dwellings. At the far end now is part of the Kirkby Centre Community complex. Happily the street name has been retained.

To church on Sunday, with the help of the St Wilfrid's car pool, 1964. Church Street has since been considerably changed. The building on the immediate right has been demolished (it was once one of the many Church Street shops) and there is now a substantial car park for churchgoers.

St Wilfrid's Church Hall, 1906. Every Sunday there were packed classes of children. It was a matter of pride to maintain attendances to qualify for books at the annual prize-giving. The building in those days was much in demand for concerts throughout the year.

One of the dozens of small shops to be found in Kirkby in the 1920s, '30s and '40s selling confectionery, tobacco and general provisions. This one was at the corner of Byron Street and School Street.

Excavation of the cutting leading to the tunnel to make way for the new Robin Hood line, 1992. The keystone has just been reached. It was 1848 when the tunnel was originally opened.

Bridge over Lindley's Lane, built to take the new Robin Hood line, early 1990s.

The view from Kingsway bridge leading towards Grive's Lane level crossing.

The view from Grive's Lane level crossing. The course of the original Midland line to Station Street curves away on the right. The new Robin Hood track turns left to approach the bridge over Lindley's Lane (see p. 109).

DAYS TO REMEMBER

The last Kirkby-in-Ashfield Urban District Council Civic Service was held at St Wilfrid's, October 1973. From left to right: Paul Chadwick, head boy of Kirkby Comprehensive School, David Marquand, MP, the Venerable Brian Woodhams, Archdeacon of Newark, the Revd C.J. Young, rector of St Wilfrid's, Councillor A.H. Briggs, JP, chairman of the council, J.A. Green, clerk to the council, Kathryn Peters, Comprehensive School head girl, Mrs Green and Alderman Mrs A. Yates, Nottinghamshire County Council.

The first St Wilfrid's branch of the Mothers' Union, *c.* 1921. More than seventy-five years later this branch of the national organization is still going strong. From its inception it has continued without a break.

Women's meeting, *c.* 1890. The Revd Thomas Woodman, rector 1876–99, is in the centre of the middle row. Mrs Woodman is seated on the extreme left.

Miners' strike parade, 1922. Led by a Charlie Chaplin lookalike, it moves leisurely along Forest Road, Annesley Woodhouse. The old Badger Box can be seen in the background next to the road.

Garden party at Fryer's Farm, 1920.

Mr and Mrs Jack Attwood at one of the St Wilfrid's Festivals. Jack, a mainly self-taught painter in oils, was a regular and popular exhibitor. Over the years he has sold many of his meticulously researched pictures.

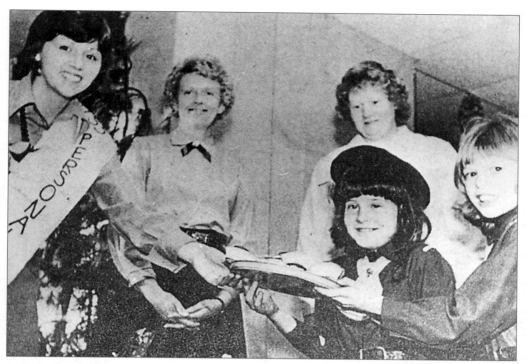

1st Annesley Woodhouse Brownies Fair, December 1975. Ashfield Youth Personality Queen, Jayne Hardwick, makes a purchase from Leigh Judson and Claire Bird.

Smiles all round from the young guests at a 1975 Christmas Party held for them at the Badger Box.

Golden Birthday, St Wilfrid's Mothers' Union, February 1971. Cutting the cake, from left to right: Mrs James (forty-three years' membership), Mrs Newton (fifty years) and Mrs Perry (forty-eight years). On the right is Mrs Jenny Young, wife of the rector.

With appropriate headgear and serious intent two boys set out in search of Robin Hood's footprints, Thieves' Wood, 1962.

An age of straw hats and sombre suits is recorded in this photograph of a carnival, 1920s. The site is the west side of Kingsway before houses were built on the land. St Thomas' Church is in the background on the right; the tent on the left obscures the houses on St Thomas's Avenue.

Kirkby Carnival in Festival of Britain year, 1951. Standing at the Station Street end of Ellis Street are Mrs Emma Rowbottom, with her son Horace on the left and Ned Harvey in top-hat and frock-coat. On display is the 'Skylon', probably a copy of an exhibit at the Festival of Britain exhibition in London.

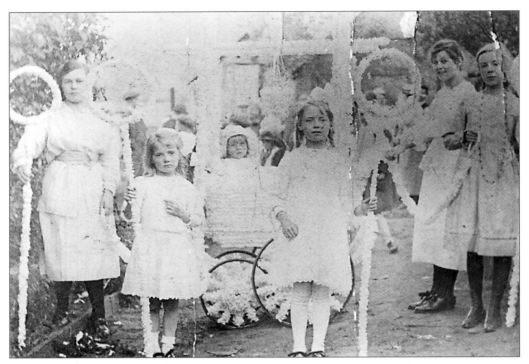

The young ladies in this carnival picture are obviously reserving their smiles until the photographer has gone, *c.* 1920.

Scott's Ice Cream vans (including one very popular horse-drawn van) were once a familiar sight in and around Kirkby. This picture was taken on Park Street in 1975.

Items of pottery sold for the St Wilfrid's Church rebuilding fund after the 1907 fire.

When the old Council Offices on Urban Road were demolished in 1986 the Kirkby Coat of Arms was built into the north wall of St Wilfrid's churchyard. In the handing-over ceremony are churchwardens Noel Kirk and Ralph Harrison, the Revd Adrian Butt, and the Chair of Ashfield Council, Mrs Glenys Thierry.

Kirkby Old Prize Band at Haddon Hall, 1951. Still winning trophies, the band, with many of its members now returned from serving with His Majesty's Forces, was much in demand both locally and further afield. Nowhere did the players acquit themselves better than when performing in the Whitsuntide Walks that were still a feature of Kirkby life in the 1950s.

A quartet of the Kirkby Old Prize Band. Standing: Len Abbott, cornet, Fred Wilkes, conductor, Peter Mayhew, cornet. Seated: Jack Graham, baritone horn, Frank Jordan, euphonium. The reputation of the quartet and its conductor was unsurpassed anywhere in the Midlands. The cups and medals displayed give support to the claim.

A party in St Thomas's Church Hall to celebrate the Coronation of Queen Elizabeth II, 1953.

Smiles all round – coupled with anticipation at the table – as another party celebrates the Queen's Coronation, this time in Acacia Avenue, Annesley Woodhouse.

The twenty-fifth anniversary party of Forest Road Methodist Chapel Women's Own, Annesley Woodhouse, 1954. Cutting the cake are Mrs R. Burgess (left), the first secretary, and Mrs A. Herrod.

Famous Cantamus all-girl choir, with conductor Pamela Cook (front, left) pays a visit to St Wilfrid's. This Mansfield choir, winner of the prestigious BBC–Sainsbury Choir of the Year competition in 1986 and 1994, was recently named Choir of the World at the famous Llangollen International Musical Eisteddfod.

Obviously intent on catching sticklebacks by some method of his own, this lad has chosen to fish in Lake Victoria in Kirkby Quarries, *c.* 1960. Portland Park was called the Quarries forty or fifty years ago, and it was always a favourite haunt in the long school holidays.

Mid-winter on the road from Larch Farm looking towards Hollinwell crossroads, early 1973.

Scenes from two of the St Wilfrid's Flower Festivals. The above picture is of the festival in 1987, and the photograph is taken at the west end looking towards the screen and the east window. Right, the stork arrives at the font bearing its precious bundle, 1989.

Kirkby Cross came tumbling down. It was hit by an articulated lorry in early December 1987. Fortunately, with skill and patience, the ancient monument was restored, much to everyone's relief.

ACKNOWLEDGEMENTS

Our grateful thanks for permission to reproduce photographs in this book go to the Rector and Parochial Church Council of St Wilfrid's Church, to numerous friends and, as previously, to the many people whose kindness and co-operation has made possible the Old Kirkby Collection.